PARTICIPANT
JOURNAL **FOUR**

SEASONS OF HOPE

M. Donna MacLeod

Ave Maria Press AVE Notre Dame, Indiana

To Erynne Lee MacLeod,

a cherished child

who loved Jesus

and now lives with him.

Scripture quotations contained herein are from the *New Revised Standard Version* of the Bible, copyright © 1993 and 1989, by the Division of Christian Education of the National Council of the Churches of Christ in the U.S.A., and are used by permission. All rights reserved.

Quotations from the English translation of the *Catechism of the Catholic Church* for the United States of America, copyright © 1994, United States Catholic Conference, Inc.—*Libreria Editrice Vaticana* are used by permission.

Founded in 1865, Ave Maria Press is a ministry of the United States Province of Holy Cross.

www.avemariapress.com

ISBN-10 1-59471-115-1   ISBN-13 978-1-59471-115-2

Cover and text design by John Carson.

Printed and bound in the United States of America.

Contents

"Seasons of Hope Prayer"

Our Father,
in this season of sorrow,
we turn to you.
Weakened with sadness,
we shed tears beyond number.
May those you send to help us
bring your love and consolation.

In this season of sorrow,
we lift up our broken hearts to you.
Heal us with your tender mercy and
make this a season of hope.
Trusting in your infinite kindness,
we ask this of you
with the Son and the Holy Spirit.
Amen.

Welcome to the
Participant Journal

Dear Brothers and Sisters in Christ Jesus,

When your loved one went home to the Lord, did you think that God was calling you to a new life in him, too? And that this new life held much more than pain and sorrow?

I had no idea what lay ahead when my daughter Erynne died. Years of caring for the dying and their families as a nurse did not prepare me for my own grief. Yet God would use the lessons I learned for the good of others. From the loss of a precious child a Christ-centered ministry to the bereaved and a hospice were born. God plans ahead. He didn't forget me, my family, or my community, and he hasn't forgotten you. He wants to console you.

Trusting in God and coming to the *Seasons of Hope* program blesses you in untold ways. The support of others who know what you go through is the first of many of God's gifts of love. Your broken heart will mend as your spirit lifts. I've seen it happen time and again.

A bible and this *Participant Journal* are all you need for the group sessions of *Seasons of Hope*. A group prayer begins the booklet and each session. Each week the facilitator will have you open to the Guidepost page for the theme, scripture citation, and activity to do before faith sharing begins.

The rest of the weekly journal is for you to use at home after the session. It generally takes about twenty minutes to complete the weekly homework—a commitment that most schedules can handle. If possible, find a quiet corner that is free of distractions. A good way to get focused is to read the week's Bible passage.

The opening comments in Looking Back give a fresh way to view the scripture story. The spiritual journey that began in the group session continues as you ask for guidance with A Prayer to Find the Way. You will read Steps Along the Path to learn how the scripture story relates to mourning and then spend time with the Reflection section to consider your situation. You can write your thoughts in the space provided under the heading, Journal Entry.

To help you cope, Moving Forward offers a Church tradition or an act of charity that generates hope. You finish the weekly journey with the Closing Prayer thanking God for the gift of consolation.

The end of the booklet has treasures of its own. Are you interested in literature and Web sites about losing a loved one? Check out Helpful Resources. Need a place to record contact information about your new friends at *Seasons of Hope*? Use the Network Directory. How about ground rules for the group? That's covered in Guide to Group Etiquette. Want to help your facilitators plan for the next season? The Season Four Survey lets you formally share your ideas.

With *Participant Journal* homework, you privately bring the trials of your loss to the Lord. You embrace his teachings, reflect on your loss, and share the painful moments so that your wounded spirit can grow strong in Christ.

May this unique way of placing Jesus Christ at the center of your grief bring you consolation.

In Christ,

M. Donna MacLeod

Session ONE

Guidepost: Point of Departure

Theme of the first session:

Last Encounter

Scripture: John 14:1–8

Marking the Route

Exercise:

   You get a chance to complete these statements in a cluster group:

- My name is _____.

- The things my family did to ease their grief were . . .

- When I was sad over losing someone dear, I would . . .

- In sad times, my family taught me that God was . . .

Notes

Home Journal: Point of Departure

Looking Back: *The Father's House*

I n this week's passage from John 14:1–8, the feast of the
Passover was underway in Jerusalem. Jesus and his
closest disciples were gathered in the city. Well aware
that religious officials wanted to arrest him, Jesus knew he
would soon leave his disciples to return to the Father.

To console the men, Jesus reminded them of their faith
in God the Father. The father figure played a tremendous
role in the culture and law of the Hebrew people. As ruler
of the household, a father was responsible for all family
members. The fatherhood of God and his covenant with
them would ensure their place in the Father's house.

Thomas admitted the fear the group had: they could not
follow Jesus home. They weren't sure where he was going.
Jesus explained that if they knew him, they would know
the way to the Father.

The Hebrew word for "to know" involves more than
grasping something intellectually. It suggests an activity
of the heart and mind, a familiarity through experience.
To know God, you must open yourself to the divine will,
acknowledge God as your source, and worship with gratitude. You know God when you keep the divine command-
ments out of love.

Like so many of us, the apostles couldn't fathom life after death. Jesus spoke of many dwelling places in the Father's house where they would live forever. He would prepare a place for them. In fact, he promised to come back to bring them to heaven. We now know that Jesus' death and resurrection opened the house of the Father to all who believe in him.

A Prayer to Find the Way

O Lord,
like your apostles,
I find it hard to imagine
what life after death truly holds,
but I believe
that my departed loved one
lives with you.
I am left behind,
but the path of mourning
is brighter because of you.
Amen.

Steps Along the Path

The truth about the heavenly kingdom of God stirs up confusion even today. Church scholars through the ages have offered the idea of heaven (the abode of God, angels, saints, and the faithful departed) as a celestial paradise and place of eternal happiness. What is lost on some is that the bliss of heaven flows from blessed unity with God that begins in this life and is perfected in the next.

Jesus and his apostles were together for quite a while. Much like you and your loved one, they wanted more time with each other even in life after death. When you lose someone dear, being left behind can be overwhelming. You might have moments when you forget that the person is gone and call out his or her name. Grief can also injure spiritual bonds and leave you feeling abandoned by God. Jesus doesn't want you to be troubled. He promised to come to his friends. How is your friendship going these days?

 Reflection

Jesus spoke of a dwelling place in the Father's house that he would prepare for his friends. Imagine Jesus actually getting some heavenly place ready. What might he do to make your loved one feel at home?

Journal Entry

When your loved one went home to the Lord, your life changed. Write to the Lord about how it feels to be left behind. Tell him how grieving affects your prayer life.

Moving Forward

If traditional prayers have become difficult for you to say during mourning, you may want to try something called "centering prayer. " It is simple to do. Find a peaceful place and take a few deep breaths to clear your mind. Then focus on the person of Jesus by repeating his name in the silence of your heart. Listen to the silence and become aware of the Lord's presence.

Closing Prayer

O loving Savior,
with a grateful heart
I remember my loved one.
I pray that, if it be your will,

_____

will dwell with you
and the Father in heaven.
I pray in your name.
Amen.

Session TWO

Guidepost: Path to Understanding

Theme of the second session:

The Garden of Gethsemane

Scripture: Mark 14:32–42

Marking the Route

Exercise:

During the allotted quiet time, imagine being in the garden where Jesus liked to pray and consider the things that the Father could help you with in your time of distress. Make a list of those requests in the space below.

Notes

Home Journal:
Path to Understanding

Looking Back: *Betrayal*

The story in Mark 14:32–42 is often referred to as the "Agony in the Garden." We can only imagine what Peter, James, and John witnessed at Gethsemane, but the account tells us that Jesus wanted them nearby as he prayed. Before praying, however, Jesus became troubled and distressed. The nature of his anguish became clear when he said his "soul" was sorrowful even to death. This spiritual struggle deepened as the fateful act of betrayal drew near.

Jesus foresaw what was coming, but his companions were clueless. In their own way, they contributed to the Lord's distress by failing to keep watch. Betrayed by his own and those who opposed his mission, Jesus prayed and surrendered his human will to the divine will of the Father—a commendable example for sorrowful souls of the ages.

A Prayer to Find the Way

O generous Jesus,
you took on the sins of humanity
out of divine love for us.
My soul is filled with sorrow
yet in you I find courage.
Help me when betrayal visits
my time of mourning.
Amen.

Steps Along the Path

If you have sat through the night at the bedside of an ill loved one, you probably can relate to the apostles who failed to keep their eyes open for the Lord. As with Peter, James, and John, the spirit may be willing, but the body is weak. Surely the apostles had good intentions when they agreed to accompany the Lord and perhaps lift him up in prayer.

Judas Iscariot, the betrayer Jesus alluded to, has intrigued scholars for centuries. Some question whether Judas forced a crisis to make Jesus perform an unmistakable sign to prove he was the Messiah. If that was Judas's purpose, he proved that good intentions aren't always what they seem.

Sometimes friends or family members think they are helpful when, in fact, their behavior is hurtful. It could be an insensitive comment, keeping their distance, or not carrying out the wishes of a loved one. Whether the failure is on a small scale like Peter, James, and John's, or larger like that of Judas, chances are you will at some point feel betrayed on your journey of mourning.

 Reflection

During grieving, it's normal to grapple with your own past behavior that might have been unsupportive. Would you do anything differently if your loved one were alive today?

Also dwell on the good intentions you acted on that met with success.

 Journal Entry

Even in a healthy relationship, miscommunication can pose a problem. Both parties may be able to forgive, but often the subconscious stores the unpleasant memory.

Write to Jesus and seek his healing touch for a hurtful memory involving you and your loved one. If none exists, give glory and thanks to God in writing.

Moving Forward

The posture we assume during prayer speaks volumes. Jesus and his followers likely prayed standing. This noble stance reflects the belief that we are made in God's likeness. In Mark's account, Jesus fell to the ground when he solemnly prayed to his Father in the Garden of Gethsemane. Whether he was prostrate or kneeling (Lk 20:41), Jesus' posture conveys complete dependence on God the Father.

As a sign of respect, we stand during the reading of the gospel and at other moments of prayer during the liturgy. We kneel during the consecration to reverence Christ present in the Eucharist, to express penitence and sorrow for sins, and to offer private prayers of petition and thanks to God.

We genuflect (bend a knee) before the tabernacle, which houses the Blessed Sacrament. We bow or genuflect before the altar, the consecrated site of the holy sacrifice of the Mass.

Each time you genuflect or bow at church this week, think of the sorrow in the Lord's heart as he fell to the ground in the Garden of Gethsemane.

Closing Prayer

Lord Jesus Christ,
your obedience to the Father's will
brought salvation to humanity.
I give you thanks
and humbly offer my sorrow to you,
trusting in your infinite love
and tender mercy.
Amen.

Session THREE

Guidepost: Obstacles on the Journey

Theme of the third session:

Crown of Thorns

Scripture: John 19:1–3

Marking the Route

Exercise:

During the allotted quiet time, imagine the pain of body, mind, and spirit that Jesus endured out of love for all humanity. Let the display on the table launch your thoughts.

Then write to Jesus about how you deal with the emotional and spiritual pain of your grief.

Notes

Home Journal: Obstacles on the Journey

Looking Back: *Suffering*

The passage of John 19:1–3 recollects what happened during Jesus' trial before Pilate. The crowds had demanded that Barabbas, not Jesus, be set free. Pilate was not convinced Jesus was guilty of a crime. To appease the crowd, Pilate sent him to be flogged.

Flogging, a severe punishment that often led to death in Jesus' day, was reserved for disobedient slaves or non-citizens of Rome. The criminal had to lie at the feet of a soldier and receive lashes to his bare chest and back with leather straps and/or chains studded with bones, metal, or spikes.

History indicates that Jesus was handed over for the cruelest of beatings. When blows that break bone, whips that sting, and thorns that stab through flesh were not enough to break Jesus' spirit, the soldiers resorted to mockery. Jesus endured all this before the heavy cross was laid upon his shoulders.

Jesus surely knew suffering. Can you imagine the sorrow in his divine heart as he faced his destiny at the hands of cruelty?

A Prayer to Find the Way

O Savior of my soul,
you endured suffering
that is beyond my comprehension.
In your suffering,
was your heart breaking?
My heart aches for you now,
though I know you gave
your life freely.
Help me keep you in mind
as I face grief and its trials.
Amen.

 ## Steps Along the Path

The soldiers who tortured Jesus put a crown of thorns and a cloak of purple (the color of royalty) on him to mock him and draw jeers from the hostile crowd. When you consider that purple also denotes spirituality, the fake king's cloak evokes the spiritual suffering endured by Jesus, the King of Kings.

When you lose a loved one, your spirit may be troubled with its own form of suffering. Do you carry something of that person with you to lift your spirits? A memento can help you remember the good times and lessen your fear of losing those memories. It can be something to lean on, helping you down the path of spiritual healing and growth.

Reflection

In the midst of grieving, it's hard to imagine you can get through the pain. Sorrow takes its toll and drains the energy needed for healing. Think about the resurrected Jesus. How does he appear to you? Are his wounds healed?

Journal Entry

How far have you come in healing after losing your loved one? Have you considered your progress? Writing down your thoughts helps put your experience into perspective. Just let the words flow out of you. You may be surprised at what you learn.

Moving Forward

Scripture this week reveals the brutality that Jesus suffered when he shed his blood at Calvary. During the consecration at Mass, ordinary wine made from grapes of the vine become for us the blood of Christ and ordinary bread becomes for us the body of Christ.

Next time you receive the chalice, think of the blood Jesus shed for all humanity. If the cup is not offered, remember the Lord's suffering as the priest prays the words of consecration.

Closing Prayer

O Risen Lord,
through the shedding
of your precious blood
salvation came.
I am eternally grateful
for all that you do for me.
Let my grieving bring good to others.
Amen.

Session FOUR

Guidepost: Path to Inner Healing

Theme of the fourth session:

Gift of Caring

Scripture: John 19:25–30

Marking the Route

Exercise:

Write a letter to Jesus. Let him know who has stood by you in your time of sorrow. Express your gratitude for the gift of their concern and their acts of kindness. If no one comes to mind, write about the gift of *Seasons of Hope*.

Note: Next week bring a crucifix to the session, if you have one.

Notes

Home Journal: Path to Inner Healing

Looking Back: *Infinite Thirst*

I f you read John 19:28–30 literally, it seems that Jesus was simply stating that he was thirsty. After all, he was hung on a cross to die. His parched mouth and throat signaled dehydration from loss of blood, lack of adequate fluids to drink, and the heat. He would be thirsty.

The gospel writer, however, says Jesus' complaint of thirst fulfills scripture, referring perhaps to Psalms 22 and 69 as possible sources of what was uttered. Both psalms lament the plight of the righteous sufferer who trusts God to rescue him.

Since Jesus was within minutes of dying, some feel that his "thirst" holds even greater significance for humanity. The message was so simple that it could easily be overlooked. Jesus thirsted for our love. He loved us and wants us to love him. Throughout his life, his mission existed because of this eternal love. His ardent desire and yearning for our love are a tremendous gift that brings new life to the weary.

Here's a question to ask yourself: how does losing a loved one affect your love of Jesus?

A Prayer to Find the Way

O Jesus, my redeemer,
may your thirst for my love
be quenched through my devotion
to you.
Let my sorrow find consolation
in you on the way
to spiritual healing.
Amen.

Steps Along the Path

Is there any time more troubled in life than when a painful death is upon someone? Hanging from a cross as though he were a criminal, Jesus was in excruciating pain. His swollen, bleeding body required fluids. Jesus expressed his need and someone took pity and offered a sponge soaked with wine.

That act of kindness showed compassion, the essence of the Savior himself. Even during suffering, Jesus brought out the best in others. Has suffering through your sorrow brought out the best in you?

Reflection

Jesus accomplished the greatest act of love—he gave up his life for the salvation of all who believe in him. During mourning, you may not feel lovable, but you are. Jesus chose you, and the depth of his love surpasses all understanding. Think about his love for you.

Journal Entry

Even relationships made in heaven don't always run smoothly. Losing a loved one can leave the most devout person with plenty of questions for the Lord. Write to Jesus about your grief and honestly share what is on your mind.

🍃 Moving Forward

In Jesus' final moments, he was the consummate bereavement minister. He wanted his mother Mary and his friend John to console each other. Scripture tells us they honored his plan.

This week follow the lead of Mary and John by reaching out to someone who lost a loved one. Share your concern with a visit, a phone call, a card, a letter, or an e-mail. Not only will an act of kindness make the recipient feel better, but you will feel better, too. Just try it.

Closing Prayer

O Jesus, consoler of us all,
thank you from the bottom
of my heart
for the promise of eternal life.
Your love for me is infinitely more
than I deserve.
Let my life reflect my love for you.
Amen.

Session FIVE

Guidepost: Way of Suffering

Theme of the fifth session:

Golgatha

Scripture: Mark 15:22–34

Marking the Route

Exercise:

Use the crucifix you brought from home or gaze at the one on the prayer table to reflect on the Lord's final moments. Let him speak to your heart. If you want to, write down your thoughts.

Note: Bring an item next week that symbolizes your love for the dearly departed one.

Notes

Home Journal: Way of Suffering

Looking Back: *Hurtful Words*

The crucifixion passage of Mark 15:22–34 brings us to Golgotha (skull place), a little hill located northwest of the city of Jerusalem where condemned criminals were executed. To deliver the Lord to this unholy place was a cruel gesture in itself, symbolic of the humiliation intended by those who had found him guilty of religious and political crimes.

If Jesus wanted to withdraw from the horror of the crucifixion, he could have drunk the wine laced with myrrh that would act like a narcotic to ease his pain and awareness. Yet he refused the drink, showing his total acceptance of God's will. The merciless ridicule he received at the hands of his enemies surely intensified the torture of being nailed to a cross.

The sign placed on the cross that read, "The King of the Jews" was not meant as a sign of honor and respect. As was customary, it stated the crime of the one being crucified. It made Jesus a target of contempt, inciting soldiers and passersby to scoff at him. We can only try to imagine how their insults must have pierced the tender, loving heart of our Savior.

Nearby, the chief priests and scribes smugly gossiped about Jesus, demanding that he come down from the cross. If you have ever been verbally kicked when you're down, you know how hurtful malicious words can be. The derogatory comments from a criminal beside Jesus surely added to his agony.

A Prayer to Find the Way

O loving Lord,
you suffered for us.
Give me the wisdom
to forgive those who hurt me.
I ask that kindness be the root
of all that I do.
Amen.

Steps Along the Path

Unkind words wield a sometimes surprisingly destructive power and often inflict great pain. The sting of comments you might encounter during grieving often comes from well-intentioned people, but callousness takes a toll nonetheless.

Insensitive remarks happen so commonly during bereavement that much is written about what to say and what not to say to the grieving. In fact, a huge concern of people of compassion is that they might say something offensive to a mourner. Fear keeps some from reaching out, from making a phone call or a visit that is sorely needed by both parties. Which side of the dilemma have you encountered?

 **Reflection**

Dealing with injured feelings takes energy particularly when you grieve. Since your loss, does something come to mind that hurt your feelings? Did you say something you wish you hadn't said? Now consider the circumstances. What do you think Jesus would advise you to do with your feelings?

Journal Entry

Hurtful remarks can slay the spirit. It only makes sense to bring your wounds to Jesus, the healer of the soul. Write to him about the situation you just reflected on, and listen for his wisdom in your heart.

🍃 **Moving Forward**

Suffering offers a chance to grow spiritually, although it rarely seems like a gift from God when you're in its throes. Mourning a loved one is a form of suffering that wounds the spirit.

Like Jesus on the cross, you too can call out to God for help and expect to receive it. When you are ready, let the Holy Spirit lead you beyond asking for assistance with your sorrow. Try giving God praise because he is God—the eternal source of love.

Closing Prayer

O triune God,
fountain of wisdom
and all consolation,
you alone know how
to heal my wounded heart and soul.
All glory and praise to you forever!
Amen.

Session SIX

Guidepost: Final Destination

Theme of the sixth session:

Be My Witnesses

Scripture: Acts 1:6–11

Marking the Route

Exercise:

Show the group something that reminds you of the love you shared with your departed loved one and tell why the item is special to you.

Seasons of Hope *has different seasons. Find out when the next one starts.*

Notes

Home Journal: Final Destination

Looking Back: *Patience*

The disciples wanted to know God's timetable, but this week's scripture reading (Acts 1:6–11) makes it clear that Jesus was not about to discuss the Father's plan. The disciples had to wait in hope for God's will to be done. Waiting would teach them many lessons about patience.

Jesus is the model of patience. The disciples' question to him about restoring the kingdom to Israel must have given him pause. How many times had he explained his mission to them? He came to reveal the Father's love, yet they clung to the ancient notion that the Messiah would be a political leader—someone to reestablish Israel's independence.

Instead of scolding them, Jesus promised the gift of the Holy Spirit to empower them to do God's work. The work was far from politics. By the power of the Holy Spirit, they would have faith in God; bring healing of body, mind, heart, soul, will, intellect, and emotion to God's people; and perform miracles of all kinds—a remarkable reward for people who had a hard time grasping the mission of the Messiah.

A Prayer to Find the Way

O Patient Savior,
I am like the disciples
who misunderstood your plans.
They wished for something
meant for another time.
Help me accept
the trials of mourning
with trust in you.
Amen.

Steps Along the Path

If you are willing to bear trials calmly and without complaint, you are a patient person. God molded you that way, so consider yourself blessed. What an inspiration you are for those around you!

Yet patience with oneself during mourning can be a challenge for many of us. We might accept the trials of grieving, but we usually expect them to pass more quickly. We grow impatient as time goes on. Impatience may suggest we have room for spiritual growth.

Yet grieving must run its course, and that course is unique for each person. Mourning seems like an unlikely time to learn how to be more patient, doesn't it? But what if God wants to use our grief to help us grow closer to him?

This week's scripture sheds light on the dilemma. Jesus recognized the grief and impatience of his disciples. So what did he do? He promised to send them the Holy Spirit. They would receive the power and patience (a fruit

of the Holy Spirit) to overcome their grief and carry on his mission.

How can you grow in patience? Ask Jesus to send you what you need.

Reflection

How patient are you when life is going smoothly? Are you more patient with others lately? Or has your level of tolerance for everyday inconveniences lessened? Does losing a loved one make you wonder if the heartache will ever end?

Journal Entry

With those questions in mind, write to Jesus about what you hope for these days.

Moving Forward

The resurrection of Jesus gave the disciples new hope in him. We can only imagine their thoughts as the Lord ascended into heaven, but we know they took that hope and went forth to be his witnesses to the ends of the earth. You too hope in Jesus and are called to go forth with the life you have been given.

Focus on the resurrected Lord by praying the Glorious Mysteries of the rosary. Let his ever-patient mother be your guide.

Closing Prayer

O God of patience and kindness,
thank you for the unique being
you made me
and for your generous gifts
of the Spirit.
With a grateful heart,
I wait for resurrection
from the depths of my sorrow.
Amen.

Appendix

Helpful Resources

BOOKS

Chatman, Delle, and William Kenneally. *The Death of a Parent: Reflections for Adults Mourning the Loss of a Father or Mother.* Chicago: ACTA, 2001.

Chilson, Richard. *Prayer: Exploring a Great Spiritual Practice.* Notre Dame, IN: Ave Maria, 2006.

Curry, Cathleen. *When Your Spouse Dies.* Notre Dame, IN: Ave Maria, 1990.

Dawson, Ann. *A Season of Grief: A Comforting Companion for Difficult Days.* Notre Dame, IN: Ave Maria, 2002.

Felber, Marta. *Finding Your Way After Your Spouse Dies.* Notre Dame, IN: Ave Maria, 2000.

Gilbert, Richard B. *Finding Your Way After Your Parent Dies: Hope for Grieving Adults.* Notre Dame, IN: Ave Maria, 1999.

Guntzelman, Joan. *God Knows You're Grieving: Things to Do to Help You Through.* Notre Dame, IN: Ave Maria, 2001.

Hamma, Robert M. *In Times of Grieving: Prayers of Comfort and Consolation.* Notre Dame, IN: Ave Maria, 2004.

Hickman, Martha Whitmore. *Healing After Loss: Daily Meditations for Working Through Grief.* New York: Avon Books, 1994.

Huntley, Theresa M. *Helping Children Grieve: When Someone They Love Dies.* Minneapolis: Augsburg Fortress, 2002.

Lafser, Christine O'Keeffe. *An Empty Cradle, A Full Heart: Reflections for Mothers and Fathers After Miscarriage, Stillbirth or Infant Death.* Chicago: Loyola Press, 1998.

Lambin, Helen Reichert. *The Death of a Husband: Reflections for a Grieving Wife.* Chicago: ACTA, 1999.

O'Brien, Mauryeen. *Lift Up Your Hearts: Meditations for Those Who Mourn.* Chicago: ACTA, 2000.

Rupp, Joyce. *Praying Our Goodbyes.* Notre Dame, IN: Ave Maria, 1988.

—————. *The Cup of Our Life: A Guide for Spiritual Growth.* Notre Dame, IN: Ave Maria, 1997.

—————. *Your Sorrow Is My Sorrow: Hope and Strength in Times of Suffering.* New York: Crossroad, 1999.

Stillwell, Elaine. *The Death of a Child: Reflections for Grieving Parents.* Chicago: ACTA, 2004.

Vogt, Robert. *The Death of a Wife: Reflections for a Grieving Husband.* Chicago: ACTA, 1997.

Wezeman, Phyllis Vos, and Kenneth R. Wezeman. *Finding Your Way After Your Child Dies.* Notre Dame, IN: Ave Maria, 2001.

Woods, Margolyn, and Maureen MacLellan. *Comfort for the Grieving Heart.* Notre Dame, IN: Ave Maria, 2002.

Zonnebelt-Smeege, Susan J., and Robert De Vries. *Getting to the Other Side of Grief: Overcoming the Loss of a Spouse.* Grand Rapids, MI: Baker Books, 1998.

WEB SITES

www.aarp.org/families/grief_loss/ has basic grief information from the AARP, 601 E St., Washington, DC 20049. 888-687-2277.

www.avemariapress.com has books on prayer, bereavement, and spiritual enrichment that comfort the downhearted.

www.bereavementmag.com connects to *Living With Loss Magazine: Hope and Healing for the Body, Mind, and Spirit.*

www.compassionatefriends.com has information and support for families who lose a child.

www.grieflossrecovery.com is a support site with related links.

www.griefwork.org offers pamphlets, books, videos, links to resources, and information on the National Catholic Ministry to the Bereaved, PO Box 16353, St. Louis, MO, 63125. 314-638-2638.

www.griefsong.com has unique ways to honor the death of a loved one.

www.widownet.com has information and self-help resources for, and by, widows and widowers.

Network Directory

Interacting with others of faith who understand what it means to lose a loved one gives you a chance to give and receive support. Use the space below for contact information of participants in your *Seasons of Hope* group.

Name_____

Phone Number_____

E-mail_____

Name_____

Phone Number_____

E-mail_____

Name_____

Phone Number_____

E-mail_____

Name_____

Phone Number_____

E-mail_____

Name_____

Phone Number_____

E-mail_____

Name_____

Phone Number_____

E-mail_____

Name_____

Phone Number_____

E-mail_____

Guide to Group Etiquette

A facilitator guides the faith sharing process by keeping the focus on the Lord and the questions. A facilitator doesn't teach, preach, or advise. He or she creates a safe place for you to talk about your feelings about loss and receive consolation.

You are expected to:

- come each week and make it known if you can't

- arrive on time

- treat others with respect

- share your faith story and then let others talk

- be a good listener

- keep what is shared in confidence

- be open to God touching you through others

Don't worry if tears flow. They are part of grieving. Smiles and laughter are welcome, too.

Season Four Survey

Please take a few moments to complete the sentences below. Thank you!

1. I learned about *Seasons of Hope* from

2. I think the meeting room is

3. Our meeting time is

4. The length of the weekly sessions is

5. The focus on prayer, scripture, and God is

6. Private time to write, listen to music, or read allows me to

7. I find faith sharing

8. The fellowship aspect of the program is

9. *Participant Journal* homework helps me

10. What I learned from *Seasons of Hope* is

11. When the next *Seasons of Hope* group forms, I

12. I'd also like to say

Date: _____

Name (optional): _____

Acknowledgments

My heartfelt thanks to all who helped shape the *Seasons of Hope Guidebook* and *Participant Journals,* particularly the clergy, friends, family, and bereaved who believe as I do that this work will enrich our parishes.

Sacred Heart Church of Hopedale, Massachusetts, hosted the first version of the bereavement group in the 1990s. Father Daniel R. Mulcahy, Jr. and Father Raymond M. Goodwin welcomed the ministry, Joe and Barbara Grillo helped out, and many enjoyed the sessions and asked for more.

Seasons of Hope in its present form was launched at Sacred Heart Church in Medford, Oregon, in 2004. Much refining was done thanks to my teammates and friends, Father Liam Cary and Mary Murphy who facilitated the sessions with me, and Kathy Wallis and Barbara Halvorsen who joined the team later. Special thanks also to Marie Carnegie, Cliff Downey, Joyce Farrell, Eleanor Geddes, Barbara Halvorsen, Doug Howat, Carol King, Joan Linkogle, Kathy Mannino, Marjorie Moore, Helen Puccetti, Annabelle Roberts, Sharon Roberts, and Arnold Widmer who gave valuable feedback on the program and *Participant Journal* pages they received each week. Some shared the journals with friends and family near and far, a testament to their appeal.

The enthusiasm and expertise of the Ave Maria Press professionals are greatly appreciated, especially those of Eileen Ponder, Bob Hamma, and Keri Suarez. Special thanks also to manuscript readers Linda Bowman, Dione and Larry Callahan, Meganne and Colt Duckworth, Nancy Mann, Helen Pride, and Barbara Wasnewsky for practical suggestions, and Mary Murphy and Sister Mary Pat Naumes for an eye to spiritual matters and Church doctrine.

My husband Bryan's wisdom, love, and generous spirit greatly influenced this work. I treasure the input of our daughter, Meganne, who remains a constant source of love and support, and the memory of dear Erynne whose death opened my heart to all who mourn.

M. Donna MacLeod, RN, MSN, a certified bereavement specialist and hospice professional, began *Seasons of Hope* support groups in 1990. Inspired by the loss of her youngest daughter, Erynne, and the compassionate response of her parish in New England, MacLeod felt called to minister to those who mourn.

A seasoned lecturer and facilitator, MacLeod has organized parish bereavement ministries across the country. She now volunteers for the Diocese of Orlando. A member of the local chapter of the Association for Death Education and Counseling, she also serves on the Board of Trustees for the National Catholic Ministry to the Bereaved.

She was motivated to write *Seasons of Hope Guidebook* by participants in the Oregon Seasons of Hope program who mentioned how beneficial they felt her materials could be to friends and family around the country.

MacLeod enjoys motherhood, grandparenthood, and residing in Florida and on Cape Cod with husband, Bryan. She can be reached through seasonsofhope@cfl.rr.com.